Reading Emily Dickinson in Icelandic

Eva Heisler

KORE PRESS / TUCSON / 2012

standing by women's words since 1993

Kore Press, Inc., Tucson, Arizona USA
www.korepress.org

Design by Sally Geier
Cover design by Lisa Bowden
Cover photo by Eva Heisler: detail, Haraldur Jónsson, *Counting* (2008)
Type is set in Neutra

We express our gratitude to those who make Kore Press publications
possible: The Tucson-Pima ArtsCouncil, The Arizona Commission on
the Arts, through appropriations from the Arizona State Legislature
and the National Endowment for the Arts.

ISBN-13: 978-1-888553-53-6

Library of Congress Cataloging-in-Publication Data

Heisler, Eva -
  [Poems. Selections]
  Reading Emily Dickinson in Icelandic : poems / Eva Heisler.
    pages cm
  Includes bibliographical references.
  ISBN 978-1-888553-53-6 (trade paper : alk. paper)
  I. Title.
  PS3608.E3852R43 2013
  811'.6--dc23
                        2012044602

READING

EMILY DICKINSON

IN ICELANDIC

Table of Contents

I. READING EMILY DICKINSON IN ICELANDIC

i. The Geography of Elsewhere

ii. Lover's Manual

iii. Impersonation

II. LARCENY—LEGACY—

I. Reading Emily Dickinson in Icelandic

i. The Geography of Elsewhere

Look-Out

I had boxes of paperback novels and a pair of binoculars. I was on the look-out for passage across water thick with leaves. This was what I believed: your body was both paper and boat. This was what I believed: that you were, like me, overlooked, and on the look-out. I knew what it was that you could not summon: words, and a willingness to throw them back. And you had what I could not summon: the view. You were a place. I wanted in the place, and on the boat. I was a difficult passage. You wanted the words, and to throw them back.

Map and Hand

The land is illegible. It is an emptiness that I cannot read. It is edge; it is not. I cannot see difference. It is an emptiness that I cannot read—like you. You map the emptiness because I cannot tell the difference between my feeling for the view and my feeling for you. This a hollow; that an elbow; there a—. At the sea is the sound of applause. This a hollow; that a shoulder; there a—. You are an edge, but I am not at the edge. This is ocean floor that has risen above sea level. In your hand, a map. I cannot tell the difference between map and hand.

Wind

That first winter in Iceland I didn't mind the wind. Stillness itself was winged. The wind wrapped me in an elsewhere—else the traffic of scholars and accountants. But this year, my heart flaps like a shutter against the side of a barn. This year, the wind no longer sounds like itself. I wake in the night and mistake the sound of the wind for the roar of the snow plow in Syracuse; the squeal of tires spinning on ice in Columbus; the hoot of a barn owl in Boyds; the whistle of a former lover's kettle. "Don't forget what it was like before." Lying in bed, I tell myself this. The sound of the wind engulfs me like the roar of an airplane does its passenger. "Don't forget." Remember the bottoms of your feet slippery with perspiration, and a jingle at every turn.

Rotten Shark on a Toothpick

It was March. You said, In April, I will pack the Toyota with your books. In May, I will feed you cake in the sun. In June, I will bring you a radish the size of an apple. You said, In July, we will make rhubarb jam and rhubarb bread and rhubarb soup. In August, we will fill the Toyota with driftwood from Russia. You said, In September, I will build a greenhouse with driftwood.

You promised to wash my hair and kiss the back of my neck in October. We will make an announcement in November, you said. In December, we will make leaf-bread while listening to Christmas songs on the radio. In January, you said, I will scold you for not wearing a scarf. In February, we will eat rotten shark with a toothpick. You said, Next March, I will pull out a photograph of you looking scared and I will say, I told you so; I told you I would take care of everything.

It Sounds Like a Poem

I stand at the front door. The radio is on, and I ask, What is being read? It sounds like a poem. Steinunn's cousin replies, No, it's the weather report. I stretch the sleeves of my sweater over my hands as I follow the approach of dark weather. It is a spot in the view through which I cannot see. I watch as my view of the far village, its bridge, the cliffs, dissolve. The wind is picking up—Steinunn will be home soon. Steinunn, with potatoes. Steinunn, with a paper. Steinunn, with something sweet. Steinunn with the long arms. Steinunn with a reach. I turn back to the house and an Emily Dickinson poem in Icelandic. I struggle with the Icelandic for "uncertain lease" and "uncertain grasp." I misread "to remember" as "to memorize."

When light in such a way—no, when light falls in a certain way another way far and wide both ways no way otherwise one way and the day is drawn as if wind—no, a ribbon—and a psalm makes a casket, no—a heaven. Something does something to the weather sign, no—the weathervane, and one day the change is published, and I wonder at the unlikely sight yet don't see the emerald, thinking diamond—

Smile

She speaks to me in Icelandic. She doesn't realize that I'm a foreigner. I nod; I smile. She asks a question; I smile. She thinks she knows me. She says something about Pabbi and a house on a stick. She might be a cousin of Steinunn's. I hold on to the smile; I will it to absorb the words. But the smile is a frozen pond; it deflects the words. I cannot understand and smile at the same time. The smile is duct tape across my mouth; it is something plastic and readymade that props open my mouth and keeps it closed at the same time. She says good-bye—"bless." The smile is a cupboard; I could fold myself into it. I see it in her eyes: she is baffled that I have not said even "*já.*"

Boots

The river is still, like the photograph of a river. The sky is asylum. You are unknown. I am slow. We straddle the bog's grassy domes, and you explain that these hillocks, called *þúfur*, were caused by fluctuations of freezing and thawing. You tell me that, as a child, you believed the moon could see you. You tell me that you refused to eat unless the kitchen curtains were drawn. On the way home, an observation about cotton grass flowering at roadside ditches prompts a story about consultation with a ghost specialist. She told you that you were porous, that there were hollows into which others climbed. You were to imagine yourself as a light that could not be penetrated. Outdoors, walking, you pull bits of your history as if blades of grass for me to taste. I hear about your first lover and a third and the pattern of snow on a ridge as indication of road conditions. In the house—woolen socks drying on the radiator— you are without story. I soak my feet; you rub oil into my boots.

Paper

Steinunn put paper in my mouth. I closed my mouth, and the paper turned to pulp. "We are making spit balls," she told me. I was having this dream when I heard a door slam; I drifted back to sleep—something about telephone numbers on my palms—and then the smell of haddock pulled me into cold light.

Paper, Water, Stone

"She never remembers to take the meat out of the kettle"—*no*, that can't be. The words are stones. I put them in the kettle. Steinunn reaches into her pocket and pulls out cough drops; she puts three into her mouth at once. She says, "I need sweetness." I feel the crinkle of paper as I press myself against her to study the oily darkness around her eyes, the flaking skin along her checks, on her forehead. She says it is "the dizziness again." I bring the large blue English-Icelandic / Icelandic-English dictionary into the kitchen. I show Steinunn the word "dizziness" with its Icelandic translation. "No, that's not what I mean," she says. I point to "headache" and "nausea." I try "lethargy" and "melancholy." Steinunn whispers, "Are you hungry?" Her voice trills the familiar word; the word "hungry" skips like a stone on water.

Meat

We eat dinner at Steinunn's parents. Lamb, potatoes, red cabbage. Steinunn's father asks me something in Icelandic. I don't understand the word *kjöt*. He forks the lamb and waves it in the air as if a flag. "Kjöt!" I know enough Icelandic to follow the complaint: it is Steinunn's fault that I don't recognize the word for "meat." Steinunn's mother speaks: the sentence is a knotted handkerchief and glass shards poke through embroidered initials. I ask Steinunn to translate her mother's words. Steinunn replies, "You wouldn't be interested."

Something to Finish

Steinunn's mother takes me to the flea market at the harbor. She shuffles among mugs in the shape of soccer balls; earrings made of feathers; Judy Blume in Icelandic; Bath Boutique Barbie; Working Woman Barbie; Barbie with Baby Keiko the Whale; Barbie Sassy Pony; and "Fizz Balls" advertised as "the latest in home aromatherapy." Encountering these in the States, I would have folded into myself. But in Iceland, the kitsch doesn't claim me. I finger the gaudy beads; they don't take the shape of coffins—I am here and some place else. Steinunn's mother hands me a bundle of papers tied with boot strings. She purchased the rights to thirty-seven unfinished poems. It is a gift, she says. She pats the sheaf of papers that I press to my chest to keep from blowing away. She says, It is something to finish.

Accent

Speaking English, my Icelandic lover enchants with awkward
trills. The height of a step; the length of a bench; the
depth of a cupboard: measurements are endearments.

Speaking Icelandic, Steinunn no longer charms: woolly
syllables exclude me; our private architecture disappears
and in its place stands a stall roofed with shields.

Time Difference

It is three a.m. in Ohio; I am in bed with a note pad. It is eight a.m. in Iceland, and a woman I have not yet met studies flight schedules. By four a.m., I have a start or an end—but not the middle. She takes notes in a meeting on soil conservation. By five a.m., I have a shape on paper. She puts a sugar cube on her tongue. At six a.m., I type the morning's work. She drafts a proposal to grow a new variety of berry in Iceland. At seven a.m., I eat Grape Nut Flakes for breakfast. She eats herring on dark bread for lunch. At eight a.m., I climb three flights of stairs. She puts a sugar cube on her tongue. At nine, I write program notes for three one-act plays. She labels packets of seed. At ten, I make a list of what I can do without; she makes a list of what she must do before I arrive. At eleven, I proof an article on eighteenth-century still life painting; she researches the nineteenth-century turnip.

At noon, I walk to the underground parking garage and slip into the backseat of my car to take a nap. It is five in Iceland; she walks to the post office. At one, I smooth my skirt and feel that surely I will never make it to the end of the day; she pulls on a worn pair of fleece pants. I draft yet another proposal around two as she reads the obituaries. I finish the last of the office coffee around three. She boils water for rice and listens to news of mishaps at sea. At five p.m., I idle in traffic and listen to news of a drive-by shooting; she sits at a kitchen table in the west of Iceland and looks through seven year-old issues of *Horticulture*. Around six, I try to remember what it was I had been after that morning; she polishes her boots.

It is seven p.m.; I eat Grape Nut Flakes for dinner. It is midnight in Iceland; she listens to a broadcast of the men's choir in Ísafjörður. At eight, I pace the kitchen; she sleeps. At nine, I read *The Geology of Iceland* in the bathtub; she sleeps. At ten, I make a grocery list; she sleeps. At eleven, I hem a yellow dress; she sleeps.

I re-read an ex-lover's postcard at midnight; she sleeps. At one a.m., I try to sleep by imagining a stranger's arms around me; she sleeps. At two a.m., I draft a letter; she sleeps. At three, I re-read an ex-lover's last postcard; she sleeps. She sleeps as I sew a button on an overcoat. As I sort photographs, she sleeps. She sleeps as I crumple receipts, as I kick extension cords under the bed, as I tear the sheet and begin again.

Letter

I know that you write not what you want but what you can. I have the words; you, the place. I skim the two volumes of Katherine Mansfield's collected letters, pulling details, sometimes rewriting them, but mostly not. The weather here is marvelous. Where it is not blue it is gold. A woman in red pants sweeps leaves. Down float leaves. They fall on babies and old people. This isn't about letting you know me. It is about persuading you that where it is not blue, it is gold. I do not speak of crumpled receipts and the tangle of extension cords. "You're awake!" you remarked in the autumn, as if this were sleight of hand. This isn't about letting you know me. This is about keeping you from sleep.

Summer

The summer sky is silver-cold. Tonight: rhubarb soup. Tomorrow: rhubarb bread. Next week: claw marks where the bed had been.

ii. Lover's Manual

Midwinter Feast

Tonight I can stomach the hard fish and the pickled shark, but I know myself to be an ill-tempered guest. I watch Loa, sheep head in hand, three others stacked at her plate. A man in green stands and reads from Egil's Saga. Axel stands and recites a poem to Loa. Loa stands, a trail of grease on her bodice. She answers with a string of rhymes. I poke at a singed sheep head. Each word is a small and dark room. I find neither bench nor corridor. I smell the dampness of the dirt floor, and I reach to touch peat rising on either side of my shoulder. Step up; now step down; turn around—a smell of scorched wool. This is another room, and this is the same room; and Steinunn's sigh trails just outside the door.

No leech should unleash runes save rightly he can read them

I tell friends a story from Egil's Saga.

Egil, visiting a farm, notices a woman who is near death. He ransacks her bed and finds the cause: it is a whale bone carved with runes. A love-sick neighbor tried to carve a love-spell but, not knowing what he was doing, he made the young woman ill. Egil, shaving the markings into the fire, states: *No leech should unleash runes save rightly he can read them.*

There is a point to the story; a question I want to put to my friends—

"Out of order, out of sight," you interject.

The statement is empty, not like a koan but like a kettle.

Yes, we are in the world.

When it is just the two of us, your words make the bed.

Out of bed, we are out of place; and that is the world.

Eavesdropping in Iceland

The phone rang. Steinunn answered. I couldn't understand the Icelandic but I recognized the word *strax*, meaning "right away." I heard a clatter of stainless steel and porcelain. Steinunn moved past me, hands wet. "Be back in twenty-five minutes," she said. She didn't give me a chance to ask. I wouldn't have asked. I was hard and closed with not asking. I would have told her we needed potatoes and coffee and that I wanted something sweet. It was not the call that bothered me but the color that came to Steinunn's cheeks. The sudden color—it was a shadow. She added, "Rain comes."

I couldn't see the approach of rain. I saw the figure of a woman who would bleed the color out of home field. I saw Loa's eyes and her mouth, her eyes in her mouth, and a fierce need for water. The eyes of Steinunn were in Loa's mouth, too. I was crazy with building a fence, with enlisting the help of Steinunn to lay beams. She said, "Wind from the North comes."

I tried to watch the sky for signs. I tried to understand what Steinunn was saying about "red" meaning *this* and "ravens" meaning *that*. I tried to count breaths, to keep my eyes out of the mouths of others.

Later, I overheard Steinunn talking on the phone to her aunt. I knew enough Icelandic to know that I was the one being talked about. I thought I heard the word *eyðublað*. The word means "blank form." But maybe I heard *eyðslaemi*. That word means "extravagance." Later, Steinunn insisted I was mistaken. They had been talking about Eyþór, a cousin in Copenhagen.

Shelf Life

As a child, your aim was to be invisible. If you could not see others—if you averted your eyes—then they could not see you. Today, you look at me and the look is like a bruise on wallpaper. I am exhausted by the looking. I blame you, the stranger, for no longer being strange.

We go to the library. You read the newspaper and I read the Oxford English Dictionary. I am at the entry for "shelf" (shelf life; shelf-occupant; shelf paper; shelf-room) when you want coffee. We settle at a table just vacated by a woman in zebra-print jacket. You complain that you feel like a dusty line. As you speak, you push cake crumbs into a pile. I want to say, those aren't our crumbs; they were left behind by the woman in zebra-print. You pinch the crumbs and put them in your mouth, as if you are cleaning your plate, but it's the table.

Souvenirs as Currency

In April, I filled your car with photocopied books. The sky was noisy and dark with geese on their way to Greenland. In May, I tried to read Emily Dickinson's poems in Icelandic. You dug holes for fence posts. In June, we took the ferry to the Westmann Islands. The water was silver; the sky was silver. I moved among mirrors. I could not tell the difference between my feeling for the view and my feeling for you. In July, I took notes on Egil's Saga. In August, I spotted you going through my purse. You would have found lipstick ("Barely There"), a grocery list (carrots, curry, coffee), a receipt (carrots, curry, coffee), and a State of Ohio driver's license with the photograph of a woman who did not look like me. In August, I noticed that you carried one of my to-do lists in a shirt pocket. In August, you reached into the pockets of my coat. I watched as you studied the keys (yours), coins, bookstore receipt, another from Kaffi Mokka, the gloves (yours). In August, you examined the Noxzema in the bathroom and the peanut butter in the pantry as if these were souvenirs. Not souvenirs of some place I had been, but souvenirs of the place I was.

In September, we picked late berries along the river. You made jam. I made bread. You scolded me for buying a box of aluminum foil. In October, I found you in the laundry room trying to read cramped handwriting on the back of a receipt. "It's a dream," I explained. I had remembered a dream while standing in line at the bank. You accused me of not telling you everything. I didn't know what this meant—"everything."

In November, I taught you the words "misanthrope" and "whatchamacallit." In December, you accused me of making plans that didn't include you. In January, you said, I know you have a secret. In February, you said, "Tell me the truth." It was dark, and the window mirrored two women in big sweaters and still cold. It was March. I pulled you toward me. I heard the crinkle of paper tucked in the sleeve of your fleece. I accused you of going through my papers. You do not know the difference between the draft of a poem and an invoice, I said. Tell me the truth, you ordered. Your mouth was pursed. It was a purse fat with foreign coins. It was March. You demanded the ghost of another woman. You demanded plot. You demanded a secret. This was the currency.

Face

My face was elsewhere—it was a balloon that had slipped out of reach. I don't know when it was that I'd lost my hold. Perhaps it was the push toward a house that had no door. Perhaps it was the detour among sculptures in butter. Perhaps it was the ghost horse that I tried to saddle. Don't count, I told myself. Don't count the spots. Don't count the pennies. Don't count the shoes. Don't count the cards.

Mirrors—that's what I remembered about being in the States. Mirrors in the elevator, at the post office, in the parking garage, at the grocery store. Licking stamps, looking at a menu, trying on a pair of shoes, examining a cauliflower, and then—a face. My face—an unmade bed. My face—a penny. Posting a package, there it was again—creased, hopeful.

In Iceland, I would forgo glossy surfaces. That had been the plan. But in the winter darkness, the windows became mirrors. Instead of the river, there was a face straining to see it. Instead of the neighboring farm, there was a face with eyes like fists of gray silk. I saw myself moving through a room and closing curtains. I watched the woman hovering over another; here was a face crossed by lights. There was a face trying not to look.

Feverish Children

I recognize the signs of holding thoughts as if they were feverish children. I remember sitting in the dark, the lights of passing cars sweeping through the cold room, trying to identify which child was a stone wrapped in flannel. In the basement, I re-coiled the garden hose. In the attic, I rummaged for clothes I wish I had worn. I tried to calculate when I might reach the end of the beginning and what *exactly* would be the last scene before the middle. Maybe I had reached the climax and did not recognize it, mistaking the moment for yet another coin-operated dream.

You need to listen to this: *you are not going to figure it out.*

(Yes, I know what I would have done had someone said that to me back then, back in that city where shadows sold candles door-to-door: I would have added her to my list.)

Another Life

The battered Toyota made its way between steep gray-green mountains. Neither river nor sea was visible. The sky, a wash of indigo, narrowed, and our view was drained of light as we moved into the valley. We were squeezed by the land. She said, "I've been here with you before, in another life."

Five months passed: lamb-fold time; sun month; hay time; harvest month; slaughtering month. We drove through the same valley. I remarked, "This is the valley we passed through in another life." She replied, "I don't remember." I wasn't sure *what* she didn't remember. She didn't remember walking through snow with me in fish skin shoes? Or she didn't remember having remembered an ancient excursion that included me?

In Akureyri, we parked in front of the bay and ate cheese sandwiches. Unfolding the map, I pointed to another stretch between mountains. "Maybe it was this valley." Of course I didn't believe in a past life, but I believed in her, and I wanted to know in which dark and narrow valley she claimed I had another life.

Scene-a-Rama

The curtains are drawn, and I notice that the hem is uneven: a strip of darkness between sill and linen reminds me this set is a hobbyist's project. On the coffee table is glue gun and brochure for Model Mountain-Making Supplies. A figure spins on its fourteen super-poseable points of ball-joint articulation. The hobbyist says, "You have betrayed me." I have only to stand. I have only to stride across chalk lines on parquet. I have only to take three long steps, and I could pass through this scene-a-rama. The hobbyist says, "That door is backdrop."

The Difference between "Deny" and "Refuse"

You don't understand the difference between "deny" and "refuse." I search for examples: I deny I threaded your bright stone onto a string; I refuse to thread your bright stone onto a string.

I deny I recognize her words in your mouth; I refuse to recognize her words in your mouth.

I deny I wish more than I work; I refuse to wish more than I work.

The wish, as noun, has a specific shape that I will not describe. That I describe neither brocade overhang nor loose freightcar is a failure among failures (failure of face; failure of a ballad thrust; failure of the automated teller machine).

Wish, as verb, is breath held, work interrupted—one cannot both wish and work.

I pour back the viscous ghost.

Vermillion Border

The double curve of your upper lip is pursed.

The phantom, my competition, pulls the purse strings.

The line between your lips is a property line.

Foil

You run your finger along the counter. I watch your eyes take in the neatness, and my happiness after five days of solitude. The house smells of cinnamon and lemon. Slowly, you walk through the five rooms. At dinner, as I feed you sweet potato soup and rhubarb bread, you ask, "Why don't you do this when I am home, arrange furniture, tidy the flat—you make the place nice when you are alone."

I watch the shape-shifting of your lips as they negotiate the heat of the soup. I don't notice the drape of a tablecloth or the profile of a candlestick when I am with you. Alone, I notice the way the cups sit on a ledge. With you in the house, I notice the drape of your shoulders, the turn of a neck, the sweep of your hands; I don't notice the turn of a chair or a little fat pig in porcelain. You consider the candles, head tilted as if someone whispers in your ear. You state, "You must be planning to leave."

I do not answer; any word serves as your receipt.

I listen to the groans of the yellow house as it pitches in a north wind.

I put my uneaten gypsy soup in the fridge, and I notice the jumble of foil-covered bowls. I had meant to eat leftovers while you were North. One should cook "just enough," you had scolded.

I remove aluminum foil from bowls of fish stew, curried rice, and rhubarb soup. Pieces of foil scatter across the counter, retaining the curve of the bowls they had covered. The hollow metallic forms hover on the counter—each wasteful and foreign and shaped to fit what I could not finish.

Gingham

I couldn't find the blue notebook. It wasn't with the red notebook.

I sat in a stairwell and pictured the blue notebook.

I saw the blue notebook on a white quilt: I had been conjugating verbs.

I saw the blue notebook on the front stoop: I had been trying to describe the taste of dried Icelandic moss boiled in milk.

I saw the blue notebook on a boulder at the sea; I had underlined, and then crossed out, "sky pulses lapis-blue just before dark."

I saw the blue notebook on a wobbly patio table in the corner of a gas station; I was trying to describe the color of driftwood.

I saw the blue notebook on a gingham-covered table. I was reworking a passage when I recognized a phrase that was *hers*. The notes were in my hand, but the phrase was a rival's. I was reminded of those first months after the rival's departure: I was back; that is to say, I was gone. I was that black sock draped over the side of a boat in a car park. I reworked a passage, thinking to rework the past. I was past the middle and into the rival's cupboard when I heard tires on gravel. I hid the notebook behind a box of Christmas ornaments on the top shelf of the pantry. It was not that the notebook held secrets; it was that my words were gravel—a scatter of gravel on gingham.

Fool's Errand

Tell the others, I said.

I repeated this as I drove to your mother's.

Tell Haraldur. Tell Rósa. Tell Karlotta that I served you broth made from the bones of a raven.

I drove through the valley, away from the river, along the fjord. I drove through the flatlands, through the field of birch that in winter resembled a herd of ghost horses, past a field of broken machinery.

I knew I was close to Reykjavik when I passed along a pit of sand and coasted the steep hill that brought me eye-level to the sea.

Tell them, I said. Tell them that I eat raven meat in the west of Iceland.

I listed all the family names that I could remember. Tell Steinar. Tell Halldór. Tell Hulda. Tell Maria. Tell Þóra.

I was hungry when I returned to the yellow house that careened above a bog. Two bowls of black bean soup sat on the table. I ate both. I did not bother re-heating the soup. I deserved cold soup. I should have known.

I did not know that her sky was oil.

I did not know that the house was a machine.

I did not know that her words were bobbins.

I did not know that my chic hat was a fool's cap.

Stone; Ghost; Stone

I tried to convince myself the stone was an apparition and I would find words that dissolved stoniness. But in Steinunn's world, *I* am apparition. In the pink shimmer of the summer night, I am the one sent by her grandmother; in the months of winter darkness, I am the one who unravels the sleeves of her sweater. One day I dazzle at the horizon; another, I shoulder the cold. Since I know that I am not a ghost, it must follow that the stone is not an apparition, and the ghost horse grazing at the coast is birch hammered by a north wind.

Lover's Manual

I tip the manual out from the shadow of my head and hold it in the blue Northern light. Paragraphs of wind rattle the social worker's window. I am tin. The sky is fierce. I read paragraph after paragraph of wind. I am a metal lid rolling down the street in a fishing village. There it is: clatter, in cold blue light. There it is, in black-and-white: the mystery of Steinunn mapped. Steinunn and the sea are squared in measured boxes. A sudden cartography rivals the sullen entries in a sorry-blue notebook. I had admired the frown (a symptom); I had wanted the heat of her silence (a symptom). I read description, not reason. There is madness in reason. The world is paper. The shadows are filing cabinets. Her touch is arithmetic.

To the Right of the Window

It was March. I lay on the floor of my office and studied the map of Iceland tacked to the wall. My eye traveled along the jagged coastline and I tried to summon the view at each crook. Here was black sand. Here was black rock. Here, the lighthouse. Here was the meadow where Unn the Deep-Minded lost her comb. Here, the valley of three-hundred hills. No, not the valley of three-hundred hills. Here was black sand. There, the lighthouse. I confused west with east. Iceland, upside down, was no longer place. It was a shape. It was a command. It was a hiding-place. It was a plan. It was a piece of sea-bottom above the sea.

To the Left of the Window

It was March. I remembered, as a child, standing at the window of my grandmother's bathroom. It wasn't the view from the window that drew me but a mark to the left of the window. The wall was white, but there was a spot of yellow where the paint had chipped. I liked to run a finger along the edge where white separated from yellow. The memory of that view from Grandmother's second story— leaves pressed against the window; barn; smokehouse; granite stoop from which great-grandmothers had mounted horses—required this mark. This was what I remembered as I lay on the floor of my office on the second floor of a yellow house in Iceland. It wasn't the view. It wasn't Grandmother. It was a chip in the wall.

Imagining the End (A)

I stay in the yellow house with a woman who is not well.

I stay for those moments when the woman with long reach is awake.

I stay to look at her—to be moved by the way she moves across a room and reaches to draw a curtain.

Most of the day she is rock. Late afternoon, the rock leaks water that I catch in a red bucket and, if the wind is not strong, toss in the garden.

My steps are measured. I pour. I ladle. I spoon. I do not predict. I crease. I watch the river turn from wool to silk to cardboard to tissue paper to foil to broken eggshell.

I stay in the yellow house because I like the view from the windows, because her long arms are bread-and-butter, because her sleep holds me when I wake.

Imagining the End (B)

I return to Ohio; the eighteen months in Iceland is My Past; I make a scrap-book of maps, menus, recipes, theatre tickets, postcards, postage stamps. I rework a handful of rocks into ghost stories: one, two, five. Late at night, I open a book in Icelandic to test my recall of vocabulary. I purchase insurance and take out a loan.

Imagining the End (C)

She comes to the door and says, not that she's sorry, but that she knows a hat isn't a glove; that she knows a sweet potato is not poison. She describes the angle of a landscape and the drape of cloth in such a way that I know we share a world.

Someday, any day, she will wake and the fluff and sawdust will have been carried by a wind. Someday, any day, she will wake and it will be like stepping out of wet clothes; hers, mine.

I open the door and she is in dry clothes and I know that she is no longer in sleep. She wraps herself around me and I hear—not the crinkle of my own discarded notes—but a breath that addresses, and another that undresses. I respond in Icelandic—

False Ending

I walk along the lake, up a hill and past the Swedish Embassy and a sign for "The Volcano Show." I turn left on Grundarstígur. I pass the house of red corrugated iron, and the house with green door. At the corner store, I purchase newspaper and Prince Polo. I return to my new address; the outer concrete walls, flecked with seashells and Iceland spar, glitter in late-morning sun. A large cardboard box sits at my front door. The box smells of vinegar. Inside, I find a jar of pickles, a bottle of ketchup, an empty jar of peanut butter, three empty Coca-Cola bottles, a bit of cheese in aluminum foil, a roll of aluminum foil, Brillo pads, a pizza slicer, a broken comb, and nine bobby pins. Steinunn has rid her home of evidence that a North American once inhabited the yellow house.

Elsewhere

At last, *elsewhere.*

A raven is perched on a lamp post. I stand under the raven and listen to it puff. I watch it move a purple-black head, and I wish to be a woman who could believe this is visitation. The raven lifts a leg and scratches its head like a dog; then it defecates a ribbon of white, and I step aside.

iii. Impersonation

Yellow House

I was met with the smell of a house that hadn't been opened for weeks. I heard the buzz of flies throwing themselves at windows. The front hall was filled with leaves; leaves, too, in the kitchen. I saw no bit of me until I walked to the windows. It was there, in the view from the windows, that I located myself. The house cast a shadow on the back slope. The shadow was sharp, as if turf in the shape of a house had been cut from the ground. That was the house I wanted: sharp and clean as a silhouette. I went to make a cup of tea; raisins like tiny stones rattled in the tea canister. A bag of soil sat in the sink. I found the notebook; it was there, where I had slipped it, next to the Christmas ornaments. I abandoned the house, and the view of myself at its windows.

Feet

My stomach tolerates only warm milk, the top thickened like a piece of thin leather. The hunger is a serrated cliché. I walk down the alley Fischerund, across Austurstraeti, up Bankastræti, up Skólavörðustígur, up any hill I can find, down and up again; I walk on snow, sand, seaweed, gravel, and broken glass as my galoshes slip on the pronoun "you."

Morning

It is necessary to forget a face in order to hear the creak of floorboards beneath my feet. I reach for threads caught in the splinters of a door frame. I come across frost in the wardrobe. I find another kitchen behind my kitchen. Fennel is scattered on the floor. I sweep the fennel seeds and then tip the dustpan into my teapot; I brew dust-and-fennel tea.

Triangle

I am right: I have been wronged. I rehearse the record in a fifth-floor room overlooking red rooftops and the mountain Esja. The triangular window fogs with corrections to the story. My breath smells like liquid paper.

"There's a certain Slant of poem"

I copy the Icelandic, my hands plaster-of-Paris-white and my face marble-cold. I miscopy *ljósið* [the light] as *ljóð* [poem]: "There's a certain Slant of poem, / Winter Afternoons –". From an unseen skylight, a blue Northern light enters the cubicle. I am steady, my face an unapproachable stillness. I shoulder a marbled tune. I am foreign to myself. "When the poem goes, 'tis like the Distance...." I strike out "poem." *When the light goes,* I re-copy "certain Slant." I, copyist, fail as escape artist.

Moon-Faced Irritant

A moon-faced irritant, I sit cross-legged in the corner. I have outstayed welcome. I have mistaken etiquette for friendship. I have exhausted my supply of antiperspirant. I aggravate with my shiny face that mourns the days when it was a Christmas orange. I know not to smile but still I misread lips. I hold still and grow fat. My face is a tambourine waiting to be shaken.

Impersonation

Here, in Iceland, the faces are flat. One detects family resemblance but not regret. The face asserts indifference to wind and betrayal. *No matter that she cut the ropes. No matter that the ship drifted.* A flash of teeth signals the foreign-born who cannot lean on likeness. The smile concedes, I am stranger. I set my features into a polished surface that does not pleat at the sight of others. My face is burnished absence.

To Make a Prairie in Iceland

I open the door, and north wind passes through the front hall and out the back bedroom. A bird circles the house; the vibration of wings on its downward swoop sounds like the buckling of a folk musician's saw. I stand at the front door—a woman in several ill-fitting sweaters, graying hair pulled back with red clip—watching for weather and trying to clear a path from last year to this. It is low tide, and the river is a wrinkle of brown wool.

I read Emily Dickinson in Icelandic: *Að gera slétta grund.*

"Prairie"—
two syllables that might sound like "prayer" if spoken quickly—
is a grunt in Icelandic: *grund.*

No, I am mistaken.
Grund is not "prairie."

Slétta—the word for "smoothness"—
assumes the form of "prairie."

Að gera slétta grund: "to make a prairie."

I read the first line.

After each line, I stop to pick at a thread or turn a plant.

I remove the green tablecloth and the table, its white Formica edged with blonde wood, is a sudden object.

I place a teak bowl off-center.

I remove a dusty wood candlestick from a low shelf and rub oil into the maple.

I place the candlestick next to the bowl: it pleases me, the wood forms gleaming against the cool whiteness of the table.

It pleases me: a row of Icelandic letters that shimmer between dream and tool. Nouns, unmoored.

Horses graze the front yard. Their silver necks slope like birch in the wind. I no longer recall how I came to be here, thumbing an Icelandic dictionary and listening to horses rip grass from an untended yard patched with bursts of rhubarb.

I have forgotten the sound of my name in another's throat.

Ear

In the Immigration Office, I chat with an Icelander seated on my left. As I tell her about the novel in my lap— *Substance of Forgetting*—I look into the Icelander's right ear and see a meticulously painted room, a French Baroque interior. I don't know her well enough to ask if the interior was painted in her actual ear, or if the scene is a custom-made insert.

A Guide to the Pronunciation of Icelandic

It sounds like the **t-h** in "think" but not like the **t-h** in "this."
It sounds like the **o-u** in "about" but not like the **o-u** in "house."
Similar to the **b** in "boat."
Like the **g** in "Magda" but softer.
Like the **y** in "yet."
Same as **m** in "mouth."
Same as **n** in "no."
Same as **o** in "cot."
The **f** sounds like **v.**
The **k** sounds like **g.**
The **p** sounds like **b.**
The **t** sounds like **d.**
Stands for the **i** in "bird" or the **o** in "word" but spoken with protruded lips.
Like the first **l** in "little" but not so crisp and never so dark as in "ill" or "muddle."

Shadow Sounds

I hear

insistent end-rhymes. *Jæja.*

I need to walk, to walk fast, but the weather is wet and dark. *Jæja.*
I circle the house, keeping beneath the eavesdrop as water pools
on the roof. *Jæja.*
I overhear laughter and "r's" whirring like little machines. *Jæja.*
I drift among syllables. *Jæja.*

Even the consonants, uttered as breath is inhaled or another
exhaled, sound like vowels, vowels as stalls that lead one to the
other. I can't hear word endings—a last syllable stalls—slides into
breath. I hear through the Icelandic.

I make out shadow sounds—a found sound-resemblance. Rhyme
proliferates: courteous rhyme; irreverent rhyme; tipsy rhyme;
melancholy rhyme; indifferent rhyme; obedient rhyme; appeasing
rhyme; commanding rhyme; moping rhyme; and, finally, a fit of
rhyme against rhyme.

Amma

While waiting for the bus, I scan the paper: first, I check the television schedule; then, I skim the obituaries. An elderly woman in a fluorescent orange rain parka asks about the number 6 bus. Out of habit, I reply, in Icelandic, that I don't understand Icelandic. The woman steps close and I smell the sea. "Yes, you do," she replies. She takes another step and zips my raincoat until it scrapes my chin. She says something in a stern voice but I only recognize two words: "weather" and "house" (or maybe "sea" and possibly "wool").

June 17

I walked along Pósthússtraeti. I passed a building surrounded by scaffolding and shrouded in blue netting. At Austurvöllur, a square of green where it is said that Ingólfur Arnarson grew his hay, I saw an escaped balloon in the shape of Casper the Ghost floating over the Parliament building. It was June 17: the sky was thick and the color of wet cement. I heard my name but the greeting was not for me. A cluster of aqua porta-potties like giant Fisher Price toys sat next to Coca-Cola tents selling flags and Fanta and cotton candy. A child dressed in long skirt and tasseled hat carried a balloon in the shape of a giant cell phone. I saw Steinunn walking with her niece down Bankastraeti. Her cheeks were bright with the motion. She was wearing red, a color I'd never seen on her. It wasn't Coca-Cola red; it was red-cabbage red. Steinunn placed a hand on the back of her niece's neck and lifted the weight of hair off her shoulders. I walked up Garðastraeti, down Hringbraut, and back toward my view of the sea. I heard a group of children shouting to one another, "Bless!" "Bless!"—the Icelandic for "good-bye." Bless, yellow house. Bless, river; bless, bog. Bless, pebble in my shoe. Again I heard my name but the blessing was for another.

Kilometers Stained Blue

I listen to the drumming of rain on corrugated iron. I tell myself, don't fall asleep. I fall asleep. I am in Grandmother's house, on the way to the kitchen, and I pass a wall of mailboxes in the hall. The boxes are glass-fronted with brass nameplates: *smokehouse; stables; silo; dairy.* I peer into the recesses, deep and stuffed with yellowing materials. I notice bank receipts; and manila folders labeled with my mother's maiden name. I open a mailbox, and a smoke detector sounds; the shrill beeps become the ringing of a phone. I answer, surprised to find myself awake when I hadn't known I was asleep. I hear a voice like the sound of boots on gravel.

Steinunn says I had been there, in the yellow house; she napped in the late afternoon, after work, and I came into the room, sat in the chair next to the bed, the chair with the wobble and the green back. This is a dream? I ask. "No," she repeats. "I was awake; you were here." No, I insist, I am in Reykjavik; I have been writing. Steinunn replies, "You thought you were writing." No, I say, I *was* writing. She replies, "You're modest."

The Letter "b" in the Word "Debt"

"Time is a gift." No, not really. Reprieve from month—reckoning to wander without purpose among the lamps of rooms without calendars, of scribbling outside the timesheet, is purchased by a future self: a balding woman will pay for the time a red-haired woman spent writing "debt rhymes with brunette / debt rhymes with forget / debt rhymes with unmet." Her foreign lover pronounces the "b" in *debt*.

"I want to do nothing."

No thing is winged.

Imagining the Last on the First

Lying on the couch, knees curled to chest, I follow the trumpets of Vivaldi. I want the flare of a horn in my heart, not this whine of a door in my left knee and a bit of singed wool in my palm. I wish for pestle in my fist.

I had thought all day that you were going to call. I try to remember the exact words—not so exact because the language is mine, not yours, and I realize you hadn't said you would call today, only that you would be calling in the first of the year, not on the first. I am greedy for the rest of my life to begin, the one in which I wear scarlet wool mittens and hold a hand.

You said "impeachable" when you meant "impeccable." You said, "It is not possible to misunderstand one another."

This is an old story, an impossible story; this is a story I read once, twice, three hundred and eighty-seven times. Every time I tell it, it tells me; only later do I remember that I have heard this before. The story finds me, a lonely woman with chapped lips who kisses the window and spies a reindeer.

I remember thirty-one days during which I didn't want and so wasn't wanting, each day a glass jar inside another glass jar. I lift my hair with both hands, twist, coil, and stick three pins in strategic spots to hold a heavy graying vanity.

Passage

I left Reykjavik in darkness and drove south and east into light, the only car on the Ring Road for two hours. I drove through the winding curves of a mountain pass and into a village of greenhouses; I slowed along the glow of glass houses and watched steam rising from hot springs in the distance. I passed Skógafoss and its rainbows. I passed the turn-off to Iceland's southernmost headland with its colossal arch that rises from the sea. I remembered an October nine years earlier, wandering along the outcrop in new boots and peering into copper-framed windows of the lighthouse keeper's flat.

I drove past beaches of black sand and the lava field of the Fire Priest. The glacier, at my left, licked the landscape, and I remembered a dreary winter when I read the Fire Priest's autobiography.

I slowly climbed the steep mountain Fjarðarheiði, and then I crawled down a narrow, coiled road, chasm at the left, chasm at the right, and the glitter of sea below.

I drove into Seyðisfjörður, past an eggshell-blue church and Norwegian imitation chalets imported in kits during the nineteenth-century.

I drove onto the ferry. For three days and two nights I lay in the bunk, knees curled to chest, stomach in throat, seasick-sad as the North Sea convulsed. On the last afternoon, banned from the cabin two hours before the Danish port, I sat on the floor and listened to metal carts, heaped with dirty linen, squeak in rough waters.

What I Remember

What I remember is neither the words nor the light in the kitchen but the press of a hand against my forehead. What I remember is not the color of eyes but what it felt like to be seen. What I remember is not the overstuffed luggage but the door, and you leaning against it. What I remember is not computing sums in the margins of my notebook, but three words and a grove of birch that I mistook for a herd of ghost horses. What I remember is not the new wardrobe but a fling of red and white.

"Work"

I struggle to make—not work—but "work." I have been advised to take comfort in these pegs that hold in suspension the drape. To make "work" by locating the pegs: this justifies the work, its cost. To love while mistrusting "love": this justifies the cost, its loss. I have been assured that it is neither my doing nor my undoing that I must make do with a billboard overheard and confetti underfoot. To quit the path—to trespass the unquoted—this is not even dream but "dream."

Vellum (Dream)

It has long passed since Steinunn and I walked through rows of fish heads strung together and hanging from makeshift racks to dry in the sun, since knobby shadows swung in the afternoon sun, since fish heads clacked against one another like castanets.

I eat pork and beans in Maryland with Grandmother. She reminds me that her pine floorboards had been covered in calfskin. It took years to scrape off that vellum, she says in my dream. The house was dark when I was a child but the birch trees have been cut for firewood, and Grandmother's kitchen floods with pink Icelandic light.

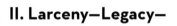

II. Larceny—Legacy—

Pilgrim

The coal damp, you must nurse the fire with paraffin,
candle-ends, sugar, margarine—anything that will burn.
On your knees, a stack of loose sheets: you "x" the
commas, place-names, *Vera*. Into the fire go snapshots
and postcards. No trappings, but a turning—*Miriam
conjugates the verb "to be."* All the bleached day and
ragged night, you pilgrim rooms stained by water and ink:

like gold thread a crack shines in
the window's upper pane;

thin fingers peel an egg.

To "spend a life"—as if a life, its years, were currency...
What does one buy with a life? A stone wrapped
in paper; words on the margins of an old map—

Autobiography of a Third Person

Congratulate yourself. The silence
is pagan and lacquered. Most becoming,
this adoption of the voices of others
to safeguard the first person—its lisp.
Lovely third: reckless third: unrepentant third:
tell me what to say so that "I" may say nothing.
You fret over the journals of Virginia Woolf,
the letters of Katherine Mansfield—anything
to avoid looking at the dim I.
The first person burns your tongue. You crouch
in the whine of that vowel—
insist "Tell a story, but not *the* story."
The third person has written it down for you—
and you accept her secrets as your own,
address her inky (radiant) darkness
and so avoid the messy silences of your life.
Your secret is that there is no secret—
nothing dark or spectacular
separates you from the landlady
fretting over house plans and how-to books.
Even in dreams
you are fat and your ankles swollen.
Frightened of doing nothing with your life,
that "nothing" is shaped
into a black-and-white triumphant thing.

A shadow falls across the page: the first person
wants a coat, black and cut like the heroine's.
She wants a podium. In the hall
are a woman's footprints in white—
in sugar, detergent, in gun powder.

The first person leans into a window
and studies the reflection of another. You travel
from drawer to purse to cardboard suitcase.
Find a story, any story—

Into the Fire

Katherine Mansfield, 1923

Sitting on a low stool, you toss
letters into the fire. Words
jump from the flame,

curl,

blacken at your feet.
With the toe of a black shoe you push them back—

back the chatter of the dead.

Don't leave names for others to puzzle,
the ones

to come later with brooms and bleach.

      *   *   *

...three tablets, a tablespoon of syrup. It's time
to spend your gold on one hour. *Quickly*—

write

of ropes stiffened with white paint; of the flapping
oilskins of sailors—

      *   *   *

On the back of stories
you draw chimneys, gates, a cornice—you long

to sit on a stoop,
to feel behind you a house, to call out

"I must have peonies under these windows."

       *   *   *

In the mirror you see a stranger
wrapped in scarves and a shawl—even in dreams

she is cold; in dreams the stranger says, "on gossip,
on cold kisses

I have spent the long, shining hours." A flower

rots in the stranger's brain; and on her lung
is a spot the size of a fist.

She sits at your dressing table,
is filling her pockets with biscuits and rocks.

Katherine Mansfield, Italy, 1919

You change the position of your bed,
memorize a page of Chekhov—but still you can hear

the (gloomy) sea
as it sweeps the empty chambers under your house.

Oh, the times you walked upside down on the ceiling,
flashed—

You must work.

You must write of the doctor's office,
the cyclamen like wax.

—of the black coats
to whom you've whispered "twenty-seven."

Dr. Sorapure took your hand and led you to the pain,
made you touch it, the greedy

unclean flower.

You must not resist,
must eat the ill-shaped flower and its mystery.

You write that,
"mystery,"

and then look up:
the waves as they break flash with gold—

You wish to be stern,
austere,

but you want—

"Heart, lie down"—

you covet the clang of gates,
the smell of leaves and dust,

breath on one's cheek.

Virginia Woolf Reads Katherine Mansfield's Obituary

I re-read Katherine's obituary. I could never read her stories; hers were the only words I have envied. "Try to penetrate," I write. I write, but into a dumb light. No rival knocks at my heart. No dark companion waits to collect the rags—Katherine has donned a white wreath, and death transforms her from bald and irritating into a mystery. I imagine Katherine rising from the writing table, re-arranging a bowl of wet leaves. She left behind dirty spoons and letters misaddressed. For years Katherine dogged my footsteps, a fat shadow with cheap scent. "One ought to merge," Katherine would say, and spoke of a room beneath which the sea rushed. That last time with her, in the dark room at Portland Villas, I pretended that I could not write, kept from her the work I was afraid she might expose—or ignite.

(Teed)

After you met Teed the light changed, as if you'd lived twenty-three years without being able to see the color blue. With others you strayed to the edge, inarticulate. But Teed, you knew Teed could lead you through the closets and into a clearing, a small place where you'd be safe from Mother and business and the cost of living.

You imitated Teed: slouched in doorways; wore mismatched socks; at breakfast ate sardines; refused dinner. You held books and papers to your nose as if the world were a blur. You pressed your flat feet into shoes two sizes too small just to wear the same size as Teed. Oh Moy, you who loved to walk along the tracks to Seeley, how did you with those corns and raw heels?

How much easier, more satisfying, it would have been if, instead, you'd touched that shoulder, or held Teed's hand.

*   *   *

Yes, speaking was impossible—and Teed knew you were never to know what Teed meant. And Teed was never to see the rooms in which you spoke. Again Teed said it was no good going on, and you agreed, not opening your eyes.

*   *   *

You write your name. You write your name again, this time the letters slanted left. You try your name in a spidery script. You take one of Teed's letters and trace the salutation, *Dear Moy*, each letter small and perfect.

You would rather be Teed writing your name, sitting at Teed's table with the wobbly leg, wearing Teed's gray scarf, writing *Dear dear Moy*. If you were Teed you'd make promises and pass seconds. You'd write *enough* and *it matters*.

You try writing your name upside down.

*   *   *

Poor Moy, worried you'll be sent back to the black-and-white...You cannot find the "x" illuminated at the edge of parting.

*   *   *

Dear Teed, Moy would like to know what it would take. Memory is a flashing light: red for teacher; yellow for Mother. She's in the yard, dead-heading roses, and this is one of those days you want to fit in, to be a part of the clap.

*   *   *

Teed gave you a name that hides what it identifies—a pair of shadows becomes a pair of swallows becomes Teed's shoulders.

In another country, plowing another's darkness, you know Teed doesn't.

Persephone in the Winter Palace

...you are slipping away
into dreams of the green swell and a variable star.

Hecate shakes you. "It's not time," she says.

> Snap the bright, unreal branch.
> Dreaming of the upper world
> will keep you in the underworld.
>
> There is to be no rescue.
>
> Not from Mother. Not from Hecate,
> or her furious daughters.
> Not from the green-eyed man
> who whispers "wait."

The ghostly vagrants toss you fire and a map.
You keep the fire,
but return their crazy directions.

Those first years here you wept at the lurid jokes...
the beating of hands and feet.

But you are not less faithful
for the godless who braid your hair,

and although you are dressed in dark, stained robes,
you are neither dark nor stained.

Among the bawdy, garrulous shades,
you are the ghost of a ghost.

You are afraid that you might never return.
That you have returned.
That you might never again touch a sunburned face.
That you might not survive this passion
for a dead man.

You fell in love with your husband
because he knew a lost language;

because his incantations and promises
resembled your dreams of God.

But you have been in this winter palace
for eleven winters,

and you have acquired neither the language
nor a shape.

You are inside the palace
but outside the door.

Corridors and anterooms
replace those vistas

which you had dreamed of finding.
No messages are tacked to the door.

"Hecate, bring me a dream I can trust."

You wanted a handsome dark house.

In your handsome dark house
you wander among the lost and abandoned. Among those
who will not let go of their names and nervous schemes,
those who fault the fire for being hot,
and those who blame the night
for the dark in their hands.

Once you believed yourself to be imprisoned,
but there are no locks here.

Only thirty-three rooms
and an apparition at every window.

Hecate spreads her blacks: "You need this."
The cross-beams and fire...the damnations...
the cross-legged, bright-legged ghost singing a requiem.

You do not want to spend your life
wishing you were someplace else.

You wish you were some place else.

And every stark, black form answers,
"Yes, we know."

And each soft shape answers,
"Yes, we know."

Eurydice

1.

I feed on grasses along the bay,
on the ninth wave,

but the hunger swells to thirty-five pounds.

Above me beckons the prophetic dark. Disturbed,
stern,

it summons me to a secret room.

But that ancient greed
pulls me to the earth—commands:

Look away. Eat the dirt.

Do not greet
the beautiful, inedible dark.

Eat the grass at your feet.

2.

Witnesses

form the names of those
who will replace me.

Memories of wheels and prayers
taunt,

mean me darkness,
mean to transfer me South.
With rope in my arms,
I lie under the hemorrhage,

unannounced.

3.

I want to forget the rags and toys and high cold arbors;
a slender life.

Ornaments
I toss into the water; white sleeves...

"Guilty,"
the waters say,

of a half-heart;
of not swimming in the sea.

No white water to forget—

Forget the silent half-hours.

Drink;
tarred heart, drink—

deliver me from the small pigs
and half-moons of a half-life.

4.

I no longer
mimic peace.

I am
that dread peace.

This repose
was not my choice,

but I now love
the absence

of ladders
and feverish angels.

Above,
voices speak

of vanishing moons.
I can hear

the rivalries of carriers
and climbers.

Blessed with a wide,

unchristened sleep,
I move

not up or down,
but across.

And no one maps the expanse.

5.

Do not forget my shoulders, how they carried the light.
Remember the morning
I fed you intimate lies. Dream of me in
the field, with hood; without—
Dream of me as a ring within this wood, as
the bridge you are about to cross—

Eurydice: Notes from the Waste Land

I was chasing after a voice
when I fell through a world

and landed

at the foot of a billboard
advertising food, lodging,

and depilatories. An artificial moon
shone on the ghosts

as they soaked their feet in bleach.
Daughters

painted lips onto their mouths—
and in greeting

mouthed "attitude."
Pink and wide,

my body
was most unlike the ghostly bodies

trying on wigs and whitening their teeth.
"Pick a body,"

they commanded. But not any.
No hips, no orbs—

and no hair behind the knees. Keep it dry.
Make it wave.

One moment
I had been chasing after a voice,

and the next
I was watching the dead whiten their teeth.

"Fear death by love,"
Hecate had warned.

Fear death by shiny surfaces and liquid diets.
Fear not apparitions,

but the passion for apparitions.

Follow us, the ghosts mouthed.
To the slippers. To the stays.

I yearned for the turning,
a returning, of the moon, of the voice,

of black stems,
of black stems tossed—

But I remembered
from my study of fairy tales

that I shouldn't speak. And I didn't—
waiting for this world

to be broken by the entrance of another
who would name me and so name

this madness.

"Rest," they advised. And I rested
in broken images,

in mirror images, among clock-faces.

The rescuer
would not be a poet

because I knew
from my study of fairy tales

that once upon another time
and underworld

it had not transformed her,
being loved by the poet,

as within this world
and upon this time

I had failed as both lover and trope—

I could not remember
the way back.

Undone I was
by the shimmer of the skeletal,

and the promise
of becoming yet another.

I was guilty
of believing in phantoms,

of trying on false lashes and fake nails,
of mouthing *la-la*.

The way out, the ghosts promised,
lay in the right gesture, the perfect cut.

The ghosts
studied my threadbare underwear

and the soiled camisole,
the silly barrette at my neck...

I hastened to explain
that I hadn't any warning;

I hadn't had time to change—

Hermione at the End of Part One

1.

One clear dark night her mother refused—
to carry the child

across bright ladders;

to carry the dim child
through fire and poppies in the sea.

Left behind to play with blocks and clay dolls,
she builds a city; calls to the wood horses—

Clay limbs
clatter as the guardians sweep the steps, the path,

sweep her mother's name into the wind—
The name

that spells d-u-s-t, say the guardians.

...the name without face—Oh, faithless name.

Was she not worth staying for,
unlovely daughter at war in the sand—

2.

Once upon a time every time she was careful.
She was careful when she stepped over,
and she was careful when she drew water.
She was careful when she remembered,
and she was careful when she filled the jugs.

Longer it was and longer it went.
It was weevils all over again
and swamp and slur and all that talent...
Lattice...lattice...lattice
clapping in the night—and cold feet.

3.

Guardians in black paper robes
pace Hermione's room, point at the corners.

"Hermione, wake up."

The walls have turned to paper,
and on the stove are beakers of ink.

It is the end of part one.
It is time to change her name—

>   (When she was thin and dizzy,
>   when she was a horse made of shine,
>   when there was weather at her feet,
>   when she was what she meant...)

"Wake, Hermione."

"Unwind the flag."

She has no flag. No story of a story
to kiss her lips.

>   She knows that it will not be known
>   what happened to her—rubs off the gold
>   was nearly that and more. More infinitives
>   than relatives between her and the w-o-r-l-d.

"Hermione, where is your mother?"

She didn't want to sail. She didn't want to turn.
She didn't want to light the lamps. She didn't want
stem, planks, daughter...inside the heart a moth.

Larceny—Legacy—

1. Reading Emily Dickinson at Twenty-Three

Picture this: a young woman sits at a conference
table in the middle of the night reading three books
in rotation: twenty minutes Elizabeth Gaskell; twenty
minutes Margaret Drabble; twenty minutes Emily
Dickinson; twenty minutes nineteenth century; twenty
minutes twentieth century; twenty minutes lyric-time.

Twenty minutes carriage dress; twenty minutes
tent dress; twenty minutes house dress.

Twenty minutes wood fire; twenty minutes
electric fire; twenty minutes Franklin stove.

She wears a red flannel shirt, Levi jeans, and
Timberland boots.

Long unwashed hair is pulled back in a braid.

Gold-framed glasses slip down her nose.

She smokes Winston cigarettes, drinks black coffee,
and reads "Lost doubly—but by contrast—most."

Some notion of "poet" floats like a spot of grease
on her glasses.

Twenty minutes parlor shutters; twenty minutes
bedroom curtains; twenty minutes door ajar.

Twenty minutes moors; twenty minutes London underground; twenty minutes broad stone step.

Twenty minutes boots; twenty minutes heels; twenty minutes bare feet.

Twenty minutes woman with twisted ankle.

Twenty minutes woman with twisted bed sheets.

Twenty minutes woman with twisted syntax.

A wheel is at the gate.

She seeks a lock of hair.

She borrows a locket.

2. New Books at Thirty-One

I read B. and I think: *this* is what I would have written had I access to leather satchels.

I would have done *just* so had I hours to read before the crackling of logs.

I hear it now: the snap that I was denied, and the turning of paper and a loosening of wool in the heat.

Those careening italicized verbs should have been mine.

I would have written *this* line and *that* had I access to ampersands and the leisure of prepositions instead of a trail of ellipses that mark the chase of absence.

I cannot bear to trace my loss in someone else's book, and I pick up the new book by G.

Spare G.

Careful G.

The lines of G: *these* would bear my name had I wind; had I porch.

The lines of G are frank like linen that displays its creases from years in cedar, a grid of care and time.

I mistook the crackle of pine for a voice but it is a sharp fold in linen.

G.—just so—*just*—had I linen; had I cedar.

3. Reading Emily Dickinson at Forty-One

Kneeling on the floor of the library, I study the manuscript facsimiles to see if I can catch poem emerge from artifact.

In my twenties, I transcribed the poet-as-lover; in my thirties, I recognized the poem-as-closet.

Now, forty, the focus is gem-tactics and the practice of sands.

This—knots [invites]—appalls [smites]—endows [erases]—shoulders [veils]—glimmers [maps]—proves [distils]—dissolves [distils]—returns [remembers]—inspects [convicts].

The difference between "foyer" and "closet" is the difference between "refuse" and "deny."

The difference between "lover" and "guest" is the difference between "guess" and "hope."

4. Drafting a Poem at Forty-Three

The poems written in my twenties were addressed to a blue-and-gold distant guest.

I could speak to no one but the one who could not answer.

The poems written in my thirties were conversations among ghosts.

The poems written in my forties are—embarrassments.

Stubborn romance is replaced by stubborn masquerade.

Someone here is ridiculous.

"Lost doubly—but by contrast—most": I repeat this as I watch the sea turn from green to gray.

I am a clump covered in Icelandic wool.

The sea moves from the color of kiwi to the color of wet concrete.

I look at the sea and I try to remember a lake in upstate New York.

The sea is nerve-gray.

The sea is gunmetal.

I have tried to write about the lake in upstate New York according to a promise made twenty-odd years ago to an arrogant girl with long unwashed braid and the daguerreotyped face of an Amherst seventeen-year-old positioned like a miner's lamp on her twenty-three-year-old forehead.

Lost doubly—but by contrast—most.

The mouth of a twenty-three-year old leers like Halloween candy lips on a forty-three year-old face, and the candy lips hiss that I am her failure; she is not mine.

5. Reading Emily Dickinson at Forty-Seven

I fall asleep and dream that the words "organ" and "margin" rhyme.

In Place of Memory the Place of Memory

Gray sweater with torn elbow; jars of honey at back door; stack of Sears Roebuck catalogues on back porch. This is from a list I made over twenty years ago. I was twenty-three, working the night shift in a psychiatric hospital. A sluggish darkness had cornered me, and I decided to record everything I could remember of my childhood. *Jugs of cider under green table; green shutters; Underwood typewriter at bottom of attic stairs.* I found the list as I was moving (again). Three folded sheets of paper had been slipped into one of those self-help books about managing money (or time, or closets). I was just past forty, tripping over tangles of extension cords and Christmas lights as I packed cutlery. I pictured my twenty-three year old self—thick braid, plaid flannel shirt, work boots—drafting a set of directions impossible to follow: *under the porch and over the woodpile and through the smokehouse.* I don't remember why it had been important to remember that the walls in my grandmother's bedroom had been blue, that the bathtub spigot didn't work, that a second refrigerator in the kitchen held empty Royal Crown Cola bottles. *Ladderback chair; ladder in the wood pile; the red seven on the black eight.* At the top of the page was the floor plan of my grandmother's house, and the details moved from room to remembered room for three-quarters of a page before they became scrambled: *dead bees in Mason jar; thermos in smoke house; croquet mallets under porch; flashlight on the mantel.*

I recorded the color of a light switch and the shape of a lampshade. I forced the memory of the color of a rug, but I couldn't force the memory of myself. At the bottom of the attic stairs, in the dirt cellar, on the back porch, under my grandmother's bed, I was nowhere to be found. That last syllable in "childhood" flickered like a silent film. It had been a cloak-and-dagger time, minus the dagger.

The forced remembering, this list-making, reminded me of the personal property inventory book an agent recommended I complete for homeowner's insurance. *Table accessories; desk accessories; room dividers. Mirrors; clocks; fire irons. Foreign stamps in paper sacks. Potatoes in the wringer washing machine. Fifty-two* TV Guides *in a wheelbarrow.* What was the replacement value should I lose the memory of the Underwood at the bottom of the attic stairs? This was loss defined by absence of knowledge. I would not know that I misplaced the memory of a red rug that smelled of cider and smoke. I would know only that I could not remember what had been at my feet.

Acknowledgments

Grateful acknowledgment is made to the editors of the following journals in which versions of some of these poems first appeared.

Bellingham Review: "Souvenirs as Currency."

Chelsea: "Eurydice."

Cobalt Review: "Morning;" "Impersonation."

Constellations: "The Autobiography of a Third Person;" "Persephone in the Winter Palace;" "Eurydice: Notes from the Waste Land"

Crazyhorse: "Look-Out;" "Map and Hand;" "Wind;" "It Sounds Like a Poem;" "Smile;" "What I Remember;" "Boots;" "Letter;" "Paper, Water, Stone;" "Something to Finish;" "Imagining the End (A);" "Imagining the End (B);" "Imagining the End (C)."

The Gettysburg Review: "Into the Fire;" "Katherine Mansfield, 1919."

Indiana Review: "(Teed)."

The Journal: "Hermione at the End of Part One."

Otoliths: "Ear" (published as "Baroque Interior" as part of the longer poem "Dreams about Art").

Poetry Northwest: "Lover's Manual."

The Prose Poem: An International Journal: "Pilgrim."

Rhino: "Midwinter Feast."

Silk Road: "To Make a Prairie in Iceland."

Spiral Orb: "Summer."

"Eurydice" was awarded the 2006 Chelsea Poetry Prize.

"Larceny—Legacy—" received the 2011 Emily Dickinson Award from the Poetry Society of America.

Eva Heisler is an art critic and poet who currently lives in Germany. Her poems have been widely published in journals including *Crazyhorse*, *The Indiana Review*, *Otoliths*, and *Poetry Northwest*. Honors include *The Nation*'s "Discovery" Award and the Poetry Society of America's Emily Dickinson Award. A Fulbright grant brought her to Iceland in 1997 where she lived for nine years, writing on Icelandic art and drafting the poems in *Reading Emily Dickinson in Icelandic*.